T0013834

THE
PRONOUN
BOOK

of related interest

Trans Pride
A Coloring Book
Fox Fisher
ISBN 978 1 78775 822 3
eISBN 978 1 78775 823 0

Are You a Boy or Are You a Girl?
Sarah Savage and Fox Fisher
Illustrated by Fox Fisher
ISBN 978 1 78592 267 1
eISBN 978 1 78450 556 1

The Every Body Book
The LGBTQ+ Inclusive Guide for Kids about Sex, Gender, Bodies, and Families
Rachel E. Simon, LCSW
Illustrated by Noah Grigni
ISBN 978 1 78775 173 6
eISBN 978 1 78775 174 3

A House for Everyone
A Story to Help Children Learn about Gender Identity and Gender Expression
Jo Hirst
Illustrated by Naomi Bardoff
ISBN 978 1 78592 448 4
eISBN 978 1 78450 823 4

She's My Dad!
A Story for Children Who Have a Transgender Parent or Relative
Sarah Savage
Illustrated by Joules Garcia
ISBN 978 1 78592 615 0
eISBN 978 1 78592 616 7

He's My Mom!
A Story for Children Who Have a Transgender Parent or Relative
Sarah Savage
Illustrated by Joules Garcia
ISBN 978 1 78775 574 1
eISBN 978 1 78775 573 4

The
PRONOUN
BOOK

SHE, HE, THEY, AND ME!

Cassandra Jules Corrigan

Illustrated by Jem Milton

Jessica Kingsley Publishers
London and Philadelphia

First published in Great Britain in 2022 by Jessica Kingsley Publishers
An Hachette Company

1

Copyright © Cassandra Jules Corrigan 2022
Illustrations copyright © Jem Milton 2022

Front cover illustration source: Jem Milton.

All rights reserved. No part of this publication may be reproduced,
stored in a retrieval system, or transmitted, in any form or by any
means without the prior written permission of the publisher, nor
be otherwise circulated in any form of binding or cover other than
that in which it is published and without a similar condition being
imposed on the subsequent purchaser.

A CIP catalogue record for this title is available from the
British Library and the Library of Congress

ISBN 978 1 78775 957 2
eISBN 978 1 78775 958 9

Printed and bound in China by Leo Paper Products Ltd

Jessica Kingsley Publishers' policy is to use papers that are natural,
renewable and recyclable products and made from wood grown
in sustainable forests. The logging and manufacturing processes
are expected to conform to the environmental regulations
of the country of origin.

Jessica Kingsley Publishers
Carmelite House
50 Victoria Embankment
London EC4Y 0DZ

www.jkp.com

For all the kids in my life: Ivan, Ivy, Braxton, Drake, Jayden, Ashlynn, Jaxon, Isaiah, Stella, Vera, Frannie, Addie, and Tanner

Pronouns are also used to refer to the **gender** a person identifies as.

Our GENDER IDENTITY is the gender we know ourselves to be.

For most people, the sex they were assigned at birth matches their gender identity. This is called being CISGENDER.

But not everyone identifies as female or male. Some people identify as

NON-BINARY.

This refers to any gender identity that is not male or female.

This includes **agender** people who don't identify with any gender; **bigender** people who identify as two or more genders either simultaneously or fluctuating between them; **genderqueer** people who identify as somewhere in between multiple genders; and **genderfluid** people who identify as different genders at different times. Non-binary people look just like anyone else, and you should never assume anyone's gender simply based on how they look.

She/her/hers, he/him/his, and they/them/theirs can be used by anyone. If you identify as a non-binary gender, you can also use she/her/hers and he/him/his.

Just like everyone has different names, different people use different pronouns to refer to themselves.

Some people are also born

INTERSEX.

This is when someone is born with a body type that does not fit typical definitions of male and female.

Someone who is intersex might identity as female, male, or as a non-binary gender, and may consider themselves to be cisgender or transgender. An intersex person may wish to use gender pronouns other than she/her/hers and he/him/his, such as they/them/theirs or a

NEO-PRONOUN

such as **ze/zir/zirs**.

"Neo" means "new," but some experts believe that neo-pronouns have been used since 1858. That was a long time ago!

Some examples of neo-pronouns include **ey/em/eir**, **fae/faer/faers**, and **xe/xem/xyr**. Neo-pronouns are usually used by trans and intersex people, but they can be used by anyone! Because there are so many types of neo-pronouns, they can seem confusing at first, but you use them just like you would any other pronoun. For example, "**Xe** brushed **xyr** hair."

Changing pronouns can be scary. But no matter what pronouns you use, those who matter most will love and support you all the same.

Using the correct pronouns for someone is an important way of showing respect and kindness, so it's important to get it right! When you use the wrong pronouns to address someone, it is called **misgendering** and can be upsetting for that person.

If you mess up and call someone by the incorrect pronouns, don't worry! Simply apologize and correct yourself and try to get it right next time.

TIPS AND RESOURCES FOR ADULTS

So, you're trying to teach kids in your life about pronouns. Congratulations! You've just made an important step toward building a more accepting and understanding future for our youth!

Teaching kids about pronouns can be a daunting task, but starting the conversation is the hardest part. I hope this book has made it a little easier. After reading this book, you and your little ones might have more questions. That's okay! Learning is a process for everyone that never ends, so it's natural not to have all the answers no matter what age you are!

In the end, the best thing you can do for your child is to set a good example. Here are some simple but effective ways you can model good pronoun and gender acceptance for the kids in your life:

- Make a point to ask for people's pronouns when you meet someone new.

- Avoid terms like "preferred pronouns." A person's correct pronouns are not "preferred"; they are mandatory!

- Encourage your child to ask questions, not make assumptions!

- Make sure you and your kids are practicing the correct pronouns for a person, even if you aren't in that person's presence. No one likes it if someone talks about them in a disrespectful manner behind their back.

- Remember: correct pronouns aren't a privilege; they are basic human decency! It isn't okay to misgender someone simply because they do something you don't agree with or to use misgendering as a punishment.

- Practice the difference between plural and singular "they." If a person uses they/them pronouns, it wouldn't be proper to say "themselves," because there is only one of them. Rather, you should say "themself."

- If you accidentally misgender someone, don't make a scene or a big deal about it. This can be very tiring for people who are frequently misgendered. Simply apologize, correct yourself, and do better next time.

- Be your child's best ally. If another adult uses the wrong pronouns with your child, talk to them about it. Make sure your child's teachers, babysitters, and friends' parents know that disrespecting your child by using incorrect pronouns for them will not be tolerated.

- Challenge yourself to think differently by using terms such as "sibling" or "parent" instead of "brother/ sister" or "mother/father."

- Keep learning and exploring! There is a world of constantly evolving resources out there to strengthen your skills. GLSEN and PFLAG are two great places to start!*

*GLSEN – glsen.org; PFLAG – pflag.org

PRONOUN CHART

SUBJECT	OBJECT	POSSESSIVE	REFLECTIVE
He	Him	His	Himself
She	Her	Hers	Herself
They	Them	Theirs	Themself
Xe	Xem	Xyr	Xyrself
Ze	Zir	Zir	Zirself
Fae	Faer	Faer	Faerself
Thon	Thon	Thons	Thonself
Ey	Em	Eir	Emself
Ae	Aer	Aer	Aerself
Ve	Ver/Vir	Vis	Verself/Virself
Per	Per	Per	Perself
Hu	Hum	Hus	Huself
E	Em	Eir	Emself
Zae	Zaem	Zaer	Zaemself

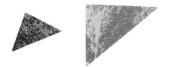

GLOSSARY OF TERMS

Agender, adj.—denoting a person who does not identify with any particular gender.

Androgyne, n.—a person whose gender identity or gender expression does not fit neatly into one gender or another.

Bigender, adj.—denoting a person who identifies with two or more genders either simultaneously or fluctuating between them.

Cisgender, adj.—denoting a person who identifies with their assigned gender at birth.

Demiboy, n.—a person who identifies partially, but not completely, as a man, boy, or as masculine, regardless of their assigned gender at birth.

Demigender, adj.—denoting a person with a partial, but not full, connection with a particular gender or gender as a whole.

Demigirl, n.—a person who identifies partially, but not completely, as a woman, girl, or as feminine, regardless of their assigned gender at birth.

Enby, n.—a non-binary person.

Genderfluid, adj.—denoting a person whose gender identity is fluid and changes.

Genderflux, adj.—an umbrella term for gender identities in which a person's gender or the intensity of a person's gender fluctuates over time.

Gender Non-conforming, adj.—denoting a person, either cisgender or transgender, whose gender expression does not line up with the societal expectations of their assigned gender at birth.

Genderqueer, adj.—denoting a person who does not subscribe to traditional gender distinctions, but rather identifies with neither, both, or a mixture of male and female identities.

Intersex, adj.—denoting someone who is born with a body not easily identifiable as male or female. This is due to any of several variations in sex characteristics such as chromosomes, gonads, sex hormones, or genitals.

Multigender, adj.—denoting a person who experiences more than one gender identity.

Neutrois, adj.—denoting someone who identifies as a "neutral" or "null" gender.

Pangender, adj.—denoting a person who is not limited to one gender identity and who may experience all genders at once.

Third Gender, adj.—denoting a person who is categorized as neither male nor female, but as another gender entirely.

Trans, adj. (see also: Transgender)—denoting a person who does not identify with their assigned gender at birth.

Transfeminine, adj.—denoting a person who was assigned male at birth but identifies as feminine.

Transgender, adj. (see also: Trans)—denoting a person who does not identify with their assigned gender at birth.

Transmasculine, adj.—denoting a person who was assigned female at birth but identifies as masculine.

Two Spirit, adj.—a gender identity specific to Indigenous North Americans, which denotes that a person fulfils a traditional third gender role for their cultures.

SAMPLE LETTER FOR PARENTS OF KIDS GOING TO SCHOOL

Dear [teacher's name],

Hello! My name is [your name], and my child [child's name] will be in your class this year. [Child's name] and I are both very excited to meet you and learn with you!

I am reaching out to inform you that my child uses they/them pronouns, and we ask that you respect this in your classroom. When referring to them, please refrain from calling them he or she.

If you have any questions, please feel free to ask! You can reach me at [e-mail address] or [phone number].

Thank you!

[Your name]

SAMPLE NOTE FOR FRIENDS' PARENTS

Dear [name],

Hello! My name is [your name], and I am [Child's name]'s parent. I'm so happy that our children have become friends, and I look forward to getting to know you better!

Since our children are embarking on new adventures together, I wanted to let you know that [child's name] uses they/them pronouns. Please respect them by using the correct pronouns and teaching your child to do the same!

If you have any questions, I'd love to answer them for you! Please feel free to email me at [e-mail address] or call me at [phone number].

Thank you!

[Your name]

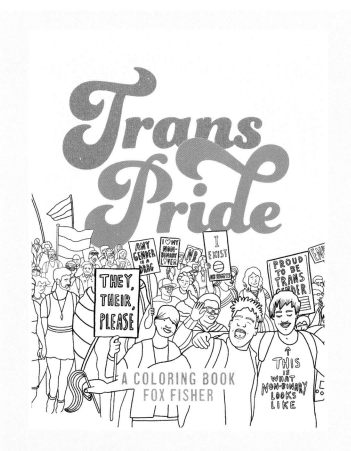

TRANS PRIDE

A Coloring Book
Fox Fisher

A fun, humorous, and beautifully illustrated coloring book celebrating the diversity and joy of trans lives. Includes over 50 individual designs to help children explore their creative expression and gender identity. The perfect gift for any child.

ISBN 978 1 78775 822 3 | eISBN 978 1 78775 823 0

ARE YOU A BOY OR ARE YOU A GIRL?

Sarah Savage and Fox Fisher
Illustrated by Fox Fisher

Tiny prefers not to tell other children whether they are a boy or girl. Tiny also loves to play fancy dress, sometimes as a fairy and sometimes as a knight in shining armor. Tiny's family doesn't seem to mind, but when they start a new school some of their new classmates struggle to understand.

ISBN 978 1 78592 267 1 | eISBN 978 1 78450 556 1

THE EVERY BODY BOOK

The LGBTQ+ Inclusive Guide for Kids about Sex, Gender, Bodies, and Families
Rachel E. Simon, LCSW
Illustrated by Noah Grigni

An illustrated LGBTQ+ inclusive kid's guide to sex, gender, and relationships education that includes children and families of all genders and sexual orientations, covering puberty, hormones, consent, sex, pregnancy, and safety.

ISBN 978 1 78775 173 6 | eISBN 978 1 78775 174 3

A HOUSE FOR EVERYONE

A Story to Help Children Learn about Gender Identity and Gender Expression
Jo Hirst
Illustrated by Naomi Bardoff

This children's picture book helps adults to explain gender identity and expression to 4–8-year-olds using simple language and engaging, diverse characters, covering the entire spectrum of gender. Includes a guide for parents and professionals, and a lesson plan.

ISBN 978 1 78592 448 4 | eISBN 978 1 78450 823 4

SHE'S MY DAD!

A Story for Children Who Have
a Transgender Parent or Relative

Sarah Savage

Illustrated by Joules Garcia

An illustrated picture book for kids age 3–7, telling the
story of Mini and her dad Haley, a transgender woman.
Mini explains why misgendering is damaging and
emphasizes the need to treat trans people with respect.

ISBN 978 1 78592 615 0 | eISBN 978 1 78592 616 7

HE'S MY MOM!

A Story for Children Who Have
a Transgender Parent or Relative

Sarah Savage

Illustrated by Joules Garcia

An illustrated picture book for kids age 3–7, telling
the story of Benjamin and his mom, David. Benjamin
speaks about pronouns, transitioning, misgendering,
family diversity, and dysphoria, and emphasizes why
we need to treat trans people with respect.

ISBN 978 1 78775 574 1 | eISBN 978 1 78775 573 4